Touching Others

COPYRIGHT

Any resemblance to actual persons,
living or dead, events, or locales is entirely coincidental.

Copyright © 2024 by Gordon G Hall

All rights reserved. No part of this book may be
reproduced or used in any manner without
written permission of the copyright owner
except for the use of quotations in a book review.

For more information, e-mail: author@lakefell.com.

First paperback edition July 2024

ISBN 78-1-0686941-2-7

www.lakefell.com

CONTENTS

COPYRIGHT v
FOREWORD xix

Casting 1

A Cancer Amongst Us 7

Apart 8

Aunt Elizabeth 9

Man-Snow 17

Fugit 19

The Pale 20

Polarisation 22

Retirement 23

Outcast 25

CONTENTS

| Cross-roads 27

| Commentary 30

| Hangers-On 33

| Void 35

| Insignificance 36

| The Tomb 37

| Other Me 39

| Hardly a breath 41

| Makes Scents 42

| The Green of Grass (1 & 2) 47

| Passing 55

| Lassitude 56

| Unstable 57

| Riddle One 62

| Riddle Two 63

CONTENTS

Riddle Three   64

Sonnet Makers   66

The Old Disease   67

The Voyeur   69

Purgatory   73

Words of Times   74

Brute   76

Stuff   78

Icarinism   81

Repairs Required   82

War Babies   87

Underpass   88

Sectioning   90

Suffice   100

Archived   101

CONTENTS

▌The Times of my Life 102

▌Her Character 104

▌Saga 105

ABOUT THE AUTHOR **109**

Touching Others

Poems and Short Stories

Gordon Hall

Crusty Books

FOREWORD

Some of the poems in this collection have been hanging around me for a considerable time - I mean 60 years or more, however most of them, and the short stories, are contemporary.

It is decidedly unfashionable these days to write poems in anything other than Free Verse. I agree that this format is liberating, and much of my current work (not part of this collection) is indeed in Free Verse. However I am old-fashioned enough to enjoy structure in poetry, and in particular the very rigid structure of the sonnet - so there are plenty of sonnets!

My original versions of both *Unstable* and *Voyeur* were, I admit , somewhat offensive and I have carried out a partial lobotomy on both so that they can be included in this 'family book'. I daresay some people may still be offended by the fun poked at religion in *Unstable* - so be it, that is your problem, not mine! And for goodness sake read to the end of *Voyeur* or you won't have a clue as to what it is all about.

There are three poems that I have classed as Riddles - although there is a fourth, *Hangers On*, which should perhaps be included. Most people get one of the three right, and

FOREWORD

many manage two. If you get all three you can bask in a self-congratulatory haze!

There are a couple of very experimental pieces - *Commentary* is not a very easy read unless you can ape the style of the late Murray Walker. *The Green of Grass* is an opportunity to see seven different poetry types written, a bit loosely, on the same subject. I suppose I could have done more, but it might have got a bit boring. I took as the subject that lovely children's question "Why is Grass Green?"

As I look through this collection I realise that an awful lot of the poems touch on the subject of death. Another, somewhat related, theme is the questioning about myself. I have tried to treat at least the latter subject with a fair dollop of humour.

The companion volume to this, *Touching Greece,* is available, again from your local bookstore, quoting the distributor as IngramSpark and the ISBN as: 978-1-0686941-0-3.

Casting

"Very well, Sir John, we take your point, but perhaps we might explore the situation just a little further?"

This insidious prying must stop. I must make it stop.

"So we are agreed that you had the overall responsibility at the time of the incident?"

The interrogator's voice slices into this island of privacy, my island of privacy.

"I do hope that you are not implying that any blame should attach itself to me."

"Nobody is apportioning any blame at this stage, indeed 'blame' is hardly the right word, but we would like to know a rather more about what actually occurred?"

The question is slinking around my back, attempting to disturb my equilibrium, trying to force me into unguarded self-betrayal. They want to see too much of me. I must preserve to myself that which is the unseen me.

"It was the merest of peccadilloes, just a small swab. "

The Board looked doubtful

I must be on my guard every day. No one must see the 'real me'. And this lot most certainly will not do so. Just watch as I wave my very own magic wand and your hero will, in one bound, be free of this inquisition.

"Of course if I had been closing up myself I would probably have left the whole thoracic cavity stuffed full of them!"

The Board exhaled. The Moment had passed. Sir John's light touch, his easy smile and his disarming manner had carried the day.

I am preserved, untouched, nothing has sneaked up too close to me, nobody has an inkling about those totally forbidden places that exist within my mind.

*

Rachael was back from the Studio by the time John arrived home. She was standing by the French windows looking out into the gathering dusk. "Hi", she said as he strode into the room, "How did it go?"

"Oh, fine", he said, chucking his evening paper on a small triangular inlaid table. "They gave poor Hartnell some grief over that swab, but she was firm and sensible about it, and quite honestly they hardly even had me in their sights over it".

"Nor should they have had", said Rachael. "After all, you weren't there at the final swab count".

"Did you get to the foundry?" said John.

TOUCHING OTHERS

Rachael's latest commission was for a bronze bust, supposedly of a noted and very dead philosopher, but actually based, fairly closely, on her husband's square-jawed features.

"I certainly did," she said, pouring rather more than half a bottle of Sancerre into a couple of glasses, "and it's going really well".

"Where's it got to now?"

"Nearly ready to melt wax," said Rachel.

She knew that the whole casting process really fascinated John. How her malleable clay model first became a rubber mould, then a thing of wax surrounded by this immensely strong, but brittle, ceramic before being melted away to provide the hollowed-out cavity for the final filling with bronze.

"Best bit coming up then," said John, playing with his still nearly full glass.

"I suppose so," said Rachel a little uncertainly.

"It's when they melt the wax out", said John, warming to his subject. "You are left with this hardened and hardly recognizable outer shell which, until they pour the bronze, conceals the perfect hollowed out image of what has been created."

Rachael sat down on the corner of the chaise. "But no one can see that", she said.

"That's what is so great about it," said John, "this rough-looking, brittle mask, which is nothing itself but which contains within itself a perfect reverse image of an identity, a beauty, a consciousness that no one can ever see. Any attempt to catch even a glimpse of this unique creation couldn't do so without causing its total destruction."

Rachel thought it best not to admit to being uneasy at the thought. "I'll feel a lot more comfortable once they have poured the bronze," she said. "After that it doesn't matter. I'll have the finished object, a bit rough but a real tangible creation that I can work on and finish off just as I want."

John shivered slightly, "That's why I prefer the hidden image. No one can access it to shape it to their will."

*

Sir John Spencer FRCS had completed his scrubbing up. He swept into Theatre hands and lower arms bare and in the classic 'prayer' style. He was clothed in green except for his white facemask and 'trademark' red surgical hat. For this, the first procedure of the morning, he had elected to wear goggles. He had been here hundreds of times before. He was in his element, the master of proceedings, the undisputed leader.

John's professional eyes flickered over his cardio-thoracic team. Good, he thought, a useful and capable group, which included Hartnell, his newly exonerated Senior House Officer. Today's list was not demanding and he should get through it swiftly enough, perhaps even have the time to meet Rachael down at the foundry. He was looking forward to it.

The team were quietly and competently busy,

everyone knew the role that they must fulfil to ensure the smooth working of the procedure. The Circulation Nurse sponged an alcohol preparation over the patient's chest to cleanse the skin and then stood back so that Hartnell could make the first incision.

In readiness for the large bleeders that would, inevitably, occur the Scrub Nurse handed John the business end of the Electro-Surgical Unit. As laid down in Operating Manual he made to test the apparatus by touching the footswitch. This would provide almost instant heat to the tip of the instrument. There was a gentle 'Whoomph'. The anaesthetist saw a shimmer of flame, but Hartnell felt the heat from the rapidly spreading fire. She jerked backwards into the Circulation Nurse who, in turn, collided with John. Her left hand hit his shoulder squeezing the remaining ethanol over his scrub shirt.

Alcohol burns intensely and invisibly, at 840 degrees Celsius. The only way to extinguish it is to smother it. The team acted swiftly, focusing entirely on the patient. The Scrub Nurse had the fire blanket over his chest killing the fire, meanwhile the Circulation Nurse fed bottles of sterile water to Hartnell to cool down the quickly reddening skin. Within a few seconds not only was the fire that had been generated from the spark of the ESU out, but the patient had been almost totally protected from its worst effects. Collectively the Team stood back with an almost audible sigh of relief and turned towards their leader.

Unseen, the fire had spread to John's alcohol-soaked scrub shirt, and thence to his mask and hat. He must have been in terrible pain, but had never uttered a word. Appraising the situation Hartnell was aware that the alcohol that had drenched her Leader was still alight. She grabbed a fire extinguisher and emptied it over the surgeon. John sank to the ground in a sitting position, back against the wall. His shirt, mask, goggles and hat were a fused mass covered in the white powder of the extinguisher. It was impossible to discern his features through the impenetrable mask.

If they did not get this moulded mass off John's head the man would not be able to breathe. Hartnell sliced at the nose area with a scalpel, to little effect. The Scrub Nurse saw that something more drastic was needed. Without a word she passed Hartnel the orthopaedic hammer and chisel.

Hartnell held the chisel against the approximate location of what had once been Sir John's red hat. She struck a light blow. The brittle fabric shattered falling as a dozen shards upon onto the theatre floor. Looking at these the Team could just make out that the inner surfaces seemed to have captured an immortalized reversed image of Sir John's facial features.

But where John's head should have been there was - nothing.

A Cancer Amongst Us

A man already dead, he stands alone.
One full paced step away from friend and foe;
That stride already made to the unknown,
His focus - where his spirit must but go.
Our careless words just widen that divide,
Lying weasels driving truth away.
Laughter falters, wishes now denied
Slip slyly from the lips of those who pray

.Yet was he ever truly one of us,
This spectre that still stays within our midst.
And is it fair that we perceive him thus,
This man who wanly waits his final tryst.

He is the fear that haunts us all, my friend.
That dread dark fear that is our lonely end.

Apart

Slip softly into the untogether,
sad-heeded duties demanding elsewhere,
making mild mock of the word 'forever',
temporary partings, such short-term despair.
One-way arrow that flies without hasting,
bringing faint hope as the eons pass by.
Distances lengthened, Present misleading
jumbled connections, emotions wrung dry.

Silky Sirens tempting the Otherwise,
slippers for toasting, and roses to prune.
Sliding in numbness to gentle demise,
a life concluded to saccharine tune.

Accept the rending, the breaking of heart.
for absence ensures that we never part.

Aunt Elizabeth

Hopfields, Kent
May 1952

    Dear Aunty Elizabeth,

    Thank you so much for the 7/6d postal order that you sent me for my birthday. It was super. I hope you are well. I am well.

    Love From
    Gerald

The Dean School, Oxford
May 1956

    Dear Auntie Elizabeth,

    Thank you so much for the 7/6d postal order that you sent me for my birthday. I will use it to buy some linseed oil for the cricket bat that Mummy and Daddy gave me. I am in the Colts now and scored 32 not out against Hartlesham School.

    I hope that you are well.

    Love
    Gerald

Windsor College,
May 1961

Dear Aunt Elizabeth,

Thank you so much for the 10/- note that you gave me for my recent birthday. I would love to tell you that I will be buying a book with it, but to be truthful I think it more likely that I will spend it at the Grubber.

I hope that you are keeping well and that you are not rattling around too much at Tattems now that you are on your own. I do so love the old house and have such fond memories of the place.

Love
Gerald

Magdelene College, Cambridge
March 1964

Dearest Aunt Elizabeth,

I so enjoyed seeing you at Christmas. It was great to get together again at Tattems. I do think that you look after the place so well, and you are such a fund of knowledge about the garden.

I am working really hard here on my Tripos. Cambridge is such a wonderful place to be and I do enjoy the studying so much.

You have always been very kind to me by

remembering my Birthday, and of course Christmas. I just wonder if you could see your way to helping me buy some of the academic books that I need. M and P are awfully good about my allowance and all that, so I don't really like to ask for any more from them. If you were able to manage £20 or so for by birthday, or perhaps a little earlier, that would be fantastic, and set me up so well.

>Your loving nephew
>Gerry

Hopfields, Kent
August 1966

>Dearest Aunt Elizabeth,

>As you can see I am back at the parental home – but only pro-tem, following the rather sudden decision to come down from Cambridge. This was a bit of a shame because I was really getting on rather well.

>I do think they were a bit unfair about that nonsense, it really was hardly my fault at all. Anyway I have high hopes of finding a job. A few quid would give me a chance to get sorted and move into the world of business so I do hope that you are set fair to divvy up for your loving nephew.

>As ever
>Gerry

Flat 2, Ellingham Crescent, London.
Aug 1967

My Dear Aunt Elizabeth,

I really appreciate your condolences. M&P were central to my life. To lose both parents at once has been something of a shock, but I have some good friends and am sure that I will pull through.

For the moment I think it best to lease Hopfields as I need to be in Town to connect with the right people. To that end I have taken a flat in a charming crescent that will suit me very well. It is a bit of an outlay and I have to tell you that whilst I am looking for work I am a bit short of funds. If you could see your way to bunking up with a couple of hundred a month it really would just see me through this lean patch.

I am so sorry not to have been able to thank you earlier for my birthday present. I appreciate that driving a large car is a little difficult for you now and can assure you that I will take the greatest care of the Aston.

As ever
Gerry

HMP Alderton,
June 1973

To Miss E Fothergill, Tattems, Kent

Bloody ridiculous them giving me three years. I know it looked a bit off, but I never smashed that girl's head into a wall, well not very hard. Now I reckon I will only be in here until just after Christmas so could you do me a big favour and get Knotty Allen to get in touch with Christy – he'll know what to do.

I have paid off most of the debts so when I am released early in the New Year I trust that you will be good for a few grand to get your favourite nephew back on the right track.

G Fothergill-Smythe
No. 2674074

Hopfields, Kent
April 1992

My Dear Aunt Betty,

How delightful of you to have remembered my birthday, and with such generosity. It seems a lifetime ago since you used to send me those postal orders.

Following your phone call I obtained a valuation of Tattems from Sidebottom and Flanders. They tell me that it is now worth just over three million pounds.

Did you cash in any of those shares I spoke to you about? If you would care to sign the enclosed Transfer form I will re-invest them for you in my name – and thus provide a small income for you

Your loving
Gerald

Flat 2, Ellingham Crescent, London.
Aug 2002

    Betty Dear,

I am so sorry not to have been down to see you at Tattems for some years. I do hope that you are still managing there. I appreciate that you are concerned about its future and I am so grateful to you for saying that it will be mine upon your death (which will be a long time yet). It will be such a pleasure to live there and cherish the old place.

I did indeed split up with Camilla – she took me for just about all the money I had, and kept Hopfields – said she needed it for Josh and Naomi, although what sort of life they have there with that awful Nigel is beyond me. I am so grateful to you for paying for the children's education, the fees are just so expensive nowadays.

As you can see I am back in the flat, at least for now. Thank goodness you bought that long leasehold. Anyway I might have some exciting news soon, and that will mean I will be moving on again

    As ever
    Gerrald

3a Kings Walk, London,
January 2004

    Dear Betts,

I do hope that they are treating you well at The Willows and that you have a rather more comfortable room.

I have moved in with Anastasia. I know she is only half my age, but honestly Betts, it will be such an asset having a Russian wife. It won't be a grand wedding but you know how Receptions get out of hand what with all those people flying over from Moscow. I really am most grateful to you for subbing up for it.

I have told Anastasia all about Tattems and how we will be living there just as soon as you can lawfully evict the present tenants. She is so excited, especially as we have to leave her flat in two years time, when she leaves her work with the Russian Embassy.

Yours ever
G

32 High Street, Clipham, Kent
August 2011
Attn Mr Gerald Fothergill-Smythe

Dear Sir,

You will be aware that we act as sole Executors in relation to the Estate of your late aunt Miss Fothergill. I regret to inform you that Miss Fothergill appears to have been living somewhat beyond her means, making many large payments to another party for some forty years or more.

To fund these growing expenses she, some years

ago, sold the property, Tattems, upon which she only held a life tenure. As I expect you have known for many years the reversionary interest has been yours under the terms of your late Grandfather's will, for which Probate was granted in 1950.

Whilst in itself the sale of Tattems would appear to have been improper I must advise you that due to the passage of time such rights as you may have possessed over the property must now be deemed extinguished.

I should also inform you that despite our advice she failed to keep up the payments on the flat in Ellingham Crescent, which has now been repossessed.

Yours faithfully,

pp Watsons, Solicitors

Man-Snow

Tread carefully
tread deeply.
Tread white to brown.
Another footprint then
another.
Bird steps – lightly tracked arrows of starvation
pointing left then
pointing right.
I follow.
Bamboo.
Collapsed, crushed flat, bending flat,
splattered flattered leaves.
Heaving fronds from weight of water,
frozen water, freezing water.
Rescue.
Hands wet, hands groping
snow-wards
released canes jacking
sky-wards
slowly, oh so slowly.
Emerging.

Shovel. Blue plastic, moulded, one piece, tough.
Heave and throw, heave and throw.
Tarmac, black, unyielding,
Scrape and twist, scrape and twist.
Snow slabs slipping.
Shovel decides, shovel dictates.
Me, a machine, its tool:
swing forward, twist left, slide, recover,
swing forward, twist left, slide, recover,
swing forward . . .
Tracks, twin tracks, beckoning onwards,
memorial lines to effort past.
Walking up tracks,
walking up effort.

Fugit

The Big Bang started it
when the arrow left its bow.
From then it was ordained that we
had just one way to go.
Out there in the Cosmos
the speed limit was set,
but neutrinos raced to Italy
and Einstein was upset.
So that which was impossible
is now a tick away,
the grandfather paradox
has us in disarray
If we outstrip our time clock
then the arrow is reversed,
we will father all our fathers
as we begat them first.
And as racing further, faster
the universe we span,
we become a singularity,
which is how we all began.

The Pale

We have strolled the forbidden garden;
My silent love and I;
We have drunk of the midnight perfumes,
And caught starlight from the sky.

We have crossed the mighty oceans;
My storm-tossed love and I.
We have ridden the foaming wave-crests,
And sucked the seas bone dry.

We have scaled the highest mountains;
My light-foot love and I.
We have climbed the highest summits,
And watched as clouds pass by.

We have wandered the darkest woodlands;
My dappled love and I.
We have counted the trees of the forest,
And howled the wild wolf's cry.

TOUCHING OTHERS

We have loved with the wildest passion;
My wanton love and I.
When you steal through my open widow
And fondle my naked thigh.

But now, Light Love, it's over,
It is time to bid me goodbye
For Moonlight shines forever
But Mortal Man must die.

Polarisation

Nailed only lightly to the whims of mind,
still residence of sanity's retreat.
Sole captive of the bleak, the black, the blind,
cruelest jailer, extolling our defeat.
Haunted by echoes of joy and laughter,
mocking phantoms, littering our wayside,
extinguishing hope of our hereafter,
tolling a melancholy eventide.

Black the dog that ensnares us in its thrall,
by indulgent snare of introspection,
stifling self, that ensures that we all
can merely skulk in our self-rejection.

Painful the journey that teaches beware
of kicking the pricks of our own despair

Retirement

Seek not just creature comforts,
where fireside slippers bring
a life that's quiet and easy
and death has lost its sting

The mind grows dull and lazy
Lulled as time crawls by
Thoughts turn back to memories
Hope and Passion die.

Your pastimes and your hobbies
Are the only stress you know
Your inward-turning vision
Means you can no longer grow

So go out and face your daemons
Push and fear and strive
Take the chances offered
Be mad, but be alive

The blood that courses through you
Runs red and thick and hot
Wounds are self-inflicted
Pain and hurt - your lot

But know this - you are living
Your challenges are true
So greet them like old comrades
It is they that make you - you!

Outcast

Sun red,
sliding down the back of nowhere,
heralding the day
that never dies completely
but lingers on
Into the darkness of the night,
chimed by glass on bottle
and wearisome creaking of beds.
Long made,
and long forgotten, coffee stains
stare up from table,
floor, and counterpane,
stark markers of a life
passed long ago.
Troubled, transitory soul,
pausing, for a moment,
contemplating cracks
to ceiling, wall and life.
An ailing, restless void.
where blackness is not bleak enough
and sanity uncertain.

fearful that the saucepan
with its cold-scramble
might promise paradise to one so wise.
Squalor claims no paradise,
just fitful rest for feeble mind
clinging grimly through the night
and, by day, no more;
mere passing memories of iron bedstead,
broken washstand, baleful dreams;
waiting for an end
that never comes.

Cross-roads

This rain was not for stopping. Water cascaded off the pavements into overwhelmed gutters causing grief to the evening traffic that sluiced its way homewards toward havens of dryness and warmth. The neon displays of the shop fronts looked out uncertainly into the blurring downpour in a vain attempt to beckon the eye.

"Penny for the Guy, Mister?"

No sooner were the words out of his mouth than the small boy was in full retreat. The tall hooded figure took no notice of the fleeing child but paused, leaving something long and curved in the doorway of one such empty, neon emblazoned establishment. It then turned towards the busy crossroads, apparently oblivious of the deluge, and seemingly captivated by the swirling reflections: red, red and amber, green, amber, red.

A large car hummed its way imperturbably citywards against the flow of traffic, unfazed by the awful conditions.

"Not the ring road, Barry".

The chauffeur bit his lip and nodded. He had intended to avoid the ring road anyway, but throughout this journey his passenger had taken it upon himself to bark directions as they approached any point of decision.

Sir Charles was not a man to be crossed, Barry knew that from bitter experience. To answer him with even a simple 'yes' or 'no' might lead to a prolonged spate of verbal abuse. Nodding was the best option.

Sir Charles had enjoyed his day, a rare occurrence outside the city. He had seen off those damned European financiers, well frankly told them to stop sticking their heads up their jacksies. Some of these lefty political types just did not 'get' the way that money was made. And Sir Charles made money.

He permitted himself the faintest of smiles when he recalled how he had seen off that frightful female who had berated him for being responsible for the unemployment that now threatened the economies of the EU. Fund managers do not create social conditions, anymore than bankers do, they react to the market, going short to provide a cushion against the Bear, and stabilizing prices through going long in commodities.

He doubted if his wife would be expecting him home tonight, and he saw no reason to surprise her. His PA would have sent that charming youth up to his penthouse suite. Pleasing young lad that, just slightly reminiscent of that chap at school, what was his name, May, that was it, Raymond May. He felt the arousal of that hard encounter in the Groves. He no longer sought sex in lavatories.

It was not, thought Barry, entirely the fault of Bankers that the country was in such a mess. But it had started with money and these big cheeses, like Sir Charles, were all in it together. They all knew each other, a cosy little international club.

The hoodie ceased its contemplation of the light sequence. It glided over to a chunky piece of street furniture, leaned over it, and made some minor adjustments. If anyone had been watching carefully they would have noticed that all the reflections were now green.

The rain continued to fall.

The large black car nearly made it across the interchange,. The driver of the number 32 bus, passing the green light saw the limousine too late. His brakes locked immediately in the foul conditions and whilst he managed to swerve slightly to his right the left side of the bus ploughed into the back of the car.

The hooded figure surveyed the resulting chaos closely to make sure that the one, intended, human had been terminated in the incident. It crossed over to the shop doorway, where the neon still flashed red, picked up its scythe and departed whence it had come.

Commentary

With this piece I am playing with this idea of 'structure' by attempting to write a story of over 500 words without any form of punctuation.

... and as the lights go out it is Hamilton who
gets the best start of the front four on the grid
getting away without wheel-spin and pulling
alongside the Red Bull on the left as they run
for the first corner but being forced almost
off the track and into the barriers by really
aggressive driving from Webber as the
Australian driver tries to defend his position
and runs wide at the hairpin as a result allowing
the McLaren through followed by Alonso
and Button with Webber now recovering from
that bit of a moment with Hamilton and
Vettel already way out on his own using all
the road and a bit more as he sweeps through
the left right of Eau Rouge without touching
the brakes then away up the hill negotiating
the easy left-hander of Raidillion and accelerating

TOUCHING OTHERS

hard on his way to the slow chicane at Les Combes
just showing the pack how it should be done
leaving his braking until the very last moment
and then easing the car over the kerbs whilst being
careful not to get on the power too soon thus
losing the rear end but disaster as Alonso brakes
ridiculously late for Rivage just clipping the rear
wing of the Hamilton McLaren and proceeding
straight to the scene of the accident. promoting
Button to second place and defending hard
against Webber as they negotiate the right-hander
of Stavelot and accelerate down through
Blanchimont pulling some five G and putting
enormous strain on the soft-compound Pirelli
tyres which are only likely to last ten laps before
we see the leaders coming in for their first change
when some may want to get the hard compound
out of the way although the cars are still carrying
a high fuel load and that means higher tyre wear
for the first half of this race although that is unlikely
to bother the fast-disappearing Vettel who has
already pulled out a lead of one point three seconds
in the first two sectors and that without using
his KERS as you can see from the on-screen graphic
which also shows DRS deployment although that
cannot be used for the first two laps the zone being
marked by the line across the track just before
Kemmel where the cars will be almost taking off as
they crest the hill but meanwhile Vettel is through

the Bus Stop and completes the first lap ahead of
Button Alonso and then a long way back Massa
who has been struggling most of the season to
match Alonsowhich surely indicates that this
will be his last season at Ferrari as next year they
are bound to want to bring in some fresh blood
to partner Alonso who I can now see nursing his
car back to the pits witha front-wheel puncture
and a damaged wing that will mean a change of
nose cone before he can re-join the race which
Vettel is now in complete control of as he rounds
La Source at the start of lap two and

the lights come on again and my mother tells me
to stop chattering to myself and go to sleep

Hangers-On

Why keep hanging on to me?
Yes, all of you!
Why not go off and do your own thing?
And soon!
What on earth is the Big Attraction?
Come on, can't any of you speak?
How came you here?
Once you were just a bunch of April Rainers
Then what happened?
OK, don't tell me,
You went to the Dogs – in a manner of speaking!
Hey you – the scrawny little one.
Can't you stop rushing around in this heat?
How about behaving more like your sexy sister?
Be cool!
Take the Veil!
As for ginger-top, did you really think
you could be supportive? Not for long!
And why has your friend got the Blues?
Could the two of you could just go for a spin and
leave me alone?

Surely, old gas-bag, if anyone is capable
of going it alone it must be you?
However if you don't slim down what can you expect?
Your sister could run rings around you!
Or like that slow brother you could play it really cool.
And why bring the sea into all this
Or was that a just a fable?
Finally, can anyone get more Way Out than you?
Possibly, but then you don't
really count!
Are you all as dumb as dust?
Just a bunch of faded old swingers? Didn't you realize that
I could never be much of a father to you?
After all without me what would you would be - nothing!
So you still think I'm your father? Nonsense the boot is on
the other foot!

Void

And the earth was Void (gen 1:2)
Look into the Void. What
do you see? You see - nothing.
There is a nothing in the Void.
You hear nothing in the Void.
No senses are in the Void.
There is no sense in the Void.
The Void is me.
I am not within it.
It is not within me.
There is just one Void.
I am the only Void.
Explore.
Explore my Void.
Sense this Void.
Feel it.
Let it sink down within
you, destructive, destroying.
Nothing is within you.
No thought, no feeling, no soul
Just Void.

Insignificance

There is only this
This small most insignificant of things
Things like this you might stand on
On not seeing such
Such is the way of the world
The world is a word too big
Big enough to lose myself in
In desperation perhaps
Perhaps in love or longing
Longing to be somewhere familiar
Somewhere familiar is what I need
Need to sustain me and provide comfort
comfort is something like desire
Desire sometimes lessens my fears
Fears entrenched in my life
My life is not at all important
Important only to me and perhaps a few others
Others have their own insignificant lives
Lives that you might stand on
On your way to your own death

The Tomb

A striven undertaking,
deepening the pitting,
colluding undertaker
heavy heaped up whole

The sum of awful reckoning
past times numbing
wilful life done passing
worlds woeful ages past

Gravity descending
to grave understanding
condolences fleeting
spurning scant souls flight

Ashes that were roses
falling not arising
chilling reaper numbering
the scything of the days

Kindred recognising
kindling no burning
steeped in dust but dusting
flecks off life descending

Nowhere now the no-thing
crawling into blackness
creeping worm-embracing
darkness, nothing, night.

Other Me

Why is there only one of Me?
Given the Space and given the Time,
More of Me might to some seem fine
Though not everyone would agree!

I'm fairly certain that I'm unique.
I'm not complaining, you understand,
In fact it makes Me feel quite grand
That I am a bit of a freak!

I wonder if I am quite alone,
Or could there, perhaps, be just one other -
My Light-years distant lost twin brother!
No, I fear that I'm on my own.

It's not that I'm sad to be on my tod,
But think of the mid-games we might play,
Me leading the other Me astray,
Whilst feeling distinctly odd!

I like sole status I must admit,
For who would be the number-one guy
If I could be He and He could be I?
In truth that worries me just a bit.

How very odd if it were true
We could chat to each other Me and Me,
With two doppelgangers for company,
Crying "One for All, and Two for Two"

But in spite of Myself it's only fair
To the rest of the world, to have to admit
That I will never in twain be split,
For the name of My game is Solitaire

Hardly a breath

A million million molecules,
of you.
Buoyant breath, lightly dancing,
absorbed by me
penetrating me.
Then, oh so reluctantly,
exhaled.
Now you,
inhale of me,
drawing my essence
deep inside you;
my bursting energy
expanding alveoli,
turning life to crimson.
Apart by a thousand miles and more.
Today just one of
those molecules
rides the currents,
and flirts its way between us,
as a kiss.

Makes Scents

OK - nose to the ground – sitting room floor – sniff – whew must have been a good party last night – subtle aroma of Claret, - St Emillion possibly – no, not sure about that - might be just a tad more fruity – but definitely a Bordeaux of some distinction?

Aha – a bit of canapé under the sofa – good these smoked salmon and creamed cheese ones – not the very best smoked salmon though - they must be on another 'economy drive' – hardly my place to start criticising although it might affect what I am given to eat.

Good news how that vacuum cleaner thingy never gets quite to the edge of the carpet so that here, next to the skirting board, there are all manner of rather nasty smelly things - let's see what we've got – hmm - a bit of fruit pastel unless I'm much mistaken - and a burnt out match – don't like that very much – and a pointed stick-object - possibly a cocktail stick – oh no, it's a toothpick - bit disgusting that one.

Just a quick snort around the fireplace - you never know - yes, no surprise in that - a plum-stone that has been shied at the fire and is now hiding behind the fire tongs - bit old I think - although sticky and with a heady aroma. - a peanut - that's strange - no peanuts last night, must go back a bit - nice thing about smell, there's a history to it – right moving on and out.

Through the French Windows into the garden – grass needs a bit of a mow, but I prefer it like this, hides tennis balls – bloody cat been here in the night – Ugh, foul scent, nothing much worse than cat shit – now Deer Slot, that's different altogether – wonderful really, such a treat.

Hello what's this - hmm met this before - nasty prickly hedgehog thing – and the fleas - I have never had so many fleas trying to jump onto my nose at one time. - I flap idly at them and leave Prickles and his hopping friends to themselves.

Now, this is interesting – paws - it's Ambrosia from next door – sweet little Blue Merle Springer – she sniffs of powder – that'll be her mistress - always cuddling her and pulling her about.

"Hi Amby, how goes it with you today?"

She never gives me a direct answer - just brushes against me and offers me her bum to smell.

"Been eating curry again?"

Her mistress likes to feed her scraps at the

end of her own meal – there's no mistaking a Vindaloo flavour to things this morning.

Normally Ambrosia is up for a game of 'chase you around the pond' – which ends up with one or both of us joining the goldfish - not today - she's definitely off colour - and there are rumblings from within her slightly distended gut - she lets one fly – now that is what I call a fart!

Gruff growling from the far side of the shed - oh no! - it's Anaconda.

Ambrosia is sniffing the air and trembling - I'm not surprised - that bag of muscles and teeth is only a picket fence away and that's hardly enough to keep an enraged Doberman at bay.

"Hi Con" I venture, in a slightly shaky voice.

The growling grows more intense and is interspersed with a number of frantic yelps – I've met those jaws before and can tell you that Con keeps his teeth well cleaned. - I do not fancy offering myself up as toothpaste so calling to Ambrosia I beat an orderly withdrawal from the immediate area.

This garden shed is a wonderful place – there's a strong smell of creosote - this tends to smother everything else - but there's so much going on in here - I carefully inspect a pile of droppings - mice, not rats - I don't much like rats, not that I'm scared of them you understand - they just don't agree with me- hah - motor mower - best avoided -

TOUCHING OTHERS

stinks of petrol and, if used recently, can give you a nasty burn – caught me out once - mind you not much danger now - it has not been used for a couple of weeks or so.

Ambrosia has got herself in amongst the rakes and hoes following some scent - possibly a shrew - her tail is wagging fit to fall off - oh bloody hell – what a crash! - she's knocked over a great swathe of tools that clatter down on our heads like policemen's truncheons - the little Blue Merle hightails it back to her side of the neighbours fence - I wait to see what sort of trouble I am in – but no one seems to have heard the racket.

I sit down next to the runner beans and contemplate - all is silence - although from time to time I can still hear Anaconda snuffling around looking for a way through the fence at the bottom of the garden - there is a light breeze from just north of east it brings with it the small of cow-shit - they must be mucking out the loose housing - bit late in the year for that - but then I suppose it has been raining a lot recently.

Enough resting – time for a bit more action - I walk slowly towards the back door - it is standing half-open - there are the most delicious smells wafting towards me - must be baking day - I can make out yeast - so that must be for the bread – and scones – ooh they smell perfect - and turkey soup –

that must be for lunch – I start to salivate - I just adore turkey soup.

The scones are out of the oven and sitting on two square metals grids on the work surface - must be a couple of dozen of them - surely she wouldn't miss just one?

I sneak cautiously up to the island unit - she's not looking - I stand up and lunge towards the nearest one - I miss - but it rolls off the grid and then off the work surface - it lands next to me on the floor - I make no mistake this time - in an instant it is in my mouth.

"Oi!"

Damn, she knows it's me - I creep stealthily around the kitchen unit keeping as close to the floor as I can.

'Oh no you don't!"

A firm pair of legs is blocking my way.

"You can't just come in here and steal scones whenever you want to!"

Bugger - I thought I had got away with that.

"And for goodness sake, Gordon, stand up straight and stop pretending that you're a bloody dog!"

The Green of Grass (1 & 2)

The Green of Grass is an experimental piece where I have addressed the subject in seven poems – all with a different structure. I took for the theme the 'silly' child-like question "Why is grass green".

One - A Villanelle
A 19 line poem in 6 stanzas of three lines and a final four line stanza. There are two refrains that appear in lines 1 and 3 of the first stanza and then alternate as the final line of the next 5 stanzas, then as lines 3 and 4 of the final stanza . There are only two rhyming words throughout the poem, rhyming for each three line stanza is ABA, and the final stanza ABAA.

> *Why does grass seem green, not blue?*
> My child, what stupid questions you pose,
> *It is green because of its hue*
>
> I ask my teacher if she can construe
> The answer. I only hope she knows
> *Why does grass seem green, not blue?*

It's the Chlorophyll that you can view
It absorbs other colours, I suppose
It is green because of its hue

My lover told me my eyes reflect true
The green of emeralds, the blue of sloes
Why does grass seem green, not blue?

I'm coloured by envy that my friends too
Know the reason but won't disclose
It is green because of its hue

The graveyard worms slide sluggishly through
The richest of grass as I decompose
Why does grass seem green, not blue?
It is green because of its hue

Two - A Haiku
Three (rhyming optional!) lines with 5 syllables, for the first, then 7, then 5 again.

    Grass is green not blue
    Because the worms passing through
    Enrich it with you

Three - A rhyming quatrain

(the second and fourth lines rhyme and are of equal syllables)

What makes the grass so green, my Daddy,
Why is it not coloured blue?
What stupid questions you ask, my child,
Have you nothing better to do?

Why is the grass so green, my Teacher,
Why is it not coloured blue?
It's the chlorophyll that's green, stupid,
The colour just shows through.

Why is the grass so green, my Tutor,
Why is it not coloured blue?
The grass absorbs other colours, dummkopf,
Leaving green as the only hue.

Why is the grass so green, my Lover,
Why is it not coloured blue?
It's the colour of your eyes, my darling,
It's just a reflection of you.

Why is the grass so green, my Child,
Why is it not coloured blue?
We coloured it in at school, my parent,
Just like they taught us to.

GORDON HALL

Why is the grass so green, my Colleagues,
Why is it not coloured blue?
It's the other side of the fence, fellow worker,
Looked at with longing by you.

Why is the grass so green, my Friend,
Why is it not coloured blue?
It's all there in your mind, Marrar,
A spliff rolled especially for you.

Why is the grass so green, my Traveller,
Why is it not coloured blue?
There's a drought out over the heath, my brother,
But the lush lands of home are in view.

Why is the grass so green, my Vicar,
Why is it not coloured blue?
The Lord ordained it so, apostate
Faith tells us it is true

Why is the grass so green, my Hospice,
Why is it not coloured blue,
'Tis the fever of you mind, dying,
There's no grass here for you.

Why is the grass so green, my Graveyard,
Why is it not coloured blue?
The turf is rich in worms, poor lost one,
The worms that feed off you.

Four- A Sestina

Six stanzas each of six lines. The last words of each line form the last words of each line in the subsequent stanza but must be re-arranged in the following order (after the first line): 615243. The final three-line stanza must contain all these words, in any order, but two per line with one forming the end of the line.

It is not that I mind the colour,
There is nothing weird about green,
It is just that no one will tell me why
It has been appropriated by grass.
It is imaginable that in another life
Lawns would grow in herbivorous blue

Such would be the impact of a garden of blue
That it would overwhelm all plants with its azure colour
Thus extinguishing most existing plant life.
Best, therefore, to stick with green,
Especially for the common or garden form of grass
Rather than the fancy stuff they develop at Wye

Which leaves the question as to why
Lawns do not come in shades of blue.
It could be the nature of grass
And the chlorophyll that provides its colour.
Mind you even this only shows as green
When sunshine brings it to life.

GORDON HALL

An artist may wish to depict rural life
In this verdant land of ours, in which case why
His does his palette hardly carry any green?
Instead it contains blobs of yellow and blue
Which he mixes to create the colour
That he needs to paint grass

So it might be that the grass,
Painted in landscapes and Still Life,
Does not comprise a single colour.
Indeed there is no reason why
Our artist cannot use just yellow and blue
And skilfully combine them to depict green

The mental image that we call green
May be essential for us to recognise grass
But may be a combination of yellow and blue.
Yet experience tells us that plant life
Is a mixture of different hues, which is why
We are so sensitive to differences in colour

So the reason why are we consider green
Rather than blue depicts plant life
Is that it is the colour we see as grass.

I admit I cheated between the first and second stanzas by equating 'Why?" with 'Wye', but that poetic licence!

TOUCHING OTHERS

Five- A Clerihew

A whimsical, four-line biographical poem (the first line usually just being the subject's name) with four lines of irregular length and meter (for comic effect) and rhyming AABB

> Gordon Graham Hall
> Will one day be no-body at all
> Worms wriggling in places obscene
> Will render the turf on top of him green

Six - A Limerick

A five line witty or nonsense poem with a strict meter and rhyming AABBA

> There was a young person I knew
> Whose lawn was a curious hue
> When asked if he'd seen
> That his grass was not green
> He said that it turned him quite blue

Seven - A Sonnet

Usually with 14 lines using iambic pentameter (dee-DAH x 5). Shakespearian Sonnet:ABABCDCDEFEFGG. There should be a 'turn' after the first octave, the final sextet forming the resolution.

Why is grass green, Daddy, why is it so?
That is a stupid thing you have asked me.
But why is it green? I really must know.
You are being silly, can you not see?
Why is grass green, Teacher? I wish I knew.
There's chlorophyll in it that's what you've seen
Absorbing the colours red, yellow, blue.
But that doesn't tell me why grass looks green

Perhaps the answer is elsewhere instead
If I learn to look closely then I see
Not through my eyes but right inside my head
That colours are mine, exclusive to me

I'll seek not for something I cannot find
But let the green grow deep within my mind

Passing

If only I knew Then that
which I know Now,
but Then is lost to my Now, even knowing
that which I now know.
If only I had Now that which I had Then,
but Now was never for knowing,
not then
Then, nothing moved, Nothing stirred, nor me.
I stood, a statue, rampaging my youth
for the lightest linger of Time,
until one day, holding hands;
the clock and I, holding hands;
we aged.
Now I linger longer, knowing what went before
and knowing that Time to come.
Secure Now and secured forever
to the inching pinching Time,
and oh so well aware,
of Nothing.

Lassitude

Send the eagles to feast afresh
upon his liver, for he took it back,
stealing it so swiftly from my belly.
That which raged within is no more,
wrenched from me, gouging an
emptiness, and leaving
but a hollow thing.
I feel the cold coming quick
upon my dreams,
extinguishing expectation,
leaving only loss.
Numbness creeps,
gorging itself upon scant
remnants of that which was,
gnawing hungrily at the innards
of my hardening shell
I cannot see a time
when the flames will return
to my belly, now that they are
chained, with Prometheus,
to that far distant rock.

Unstable

"Thank you so much, sir, will you be requiring anything further this evening?"

The dim lamplight displayed to the best of its faltering ability a sumptuously appointed room, by far the best one in this exquisitely furnished hotel. The maître d' bowed obsequiously to the tall, confident visitor as he pocketed the coins.

"Nothing further, my man. Just be sure that we are not disturbed for the next hour. I'll give you a shout before I leave."

The door closed with just the lightest of clicks and the Visitor turned to regard the rather plain woman who had arrived in the room before him.

"Good, you got my note then, thanks for coming."

"Can't think why I did. What's it all about?"

"I have some news for you, Maddy."

"Of Joe?" she enquired.

"It might just surprise you. Please don't take it the wrong way."

"Is he OK? Nothing's happened to him, has it?"

"He's going to be a father."

"What!"

"We think he might be quite good at it, being a father I mean, not the actual fathering thing. He doesn't have to do that bit."

"Who the hell are you anyway? All I have is your note asking me to be here after supper to 'hear something to my advantage'? So what is it?"

The Visitor poured out two glasses of full-blooded red wine from the decanter on the fireside table and handed one to the woman. He motioned to her to sit on one of the two richly embroidered chairs.

"Relax," he said, taking the other chair. "It's important we get this right or the whole thing will collapse around our ears."

Maddy sipped her wine gingerly. She was not used to such liquor, nor indeed to this elegant room with its well-fed fire that was keeping out the chill of the March evening. She shifted on her chair clearly ill at ease.

"One of my colleagues spoke with your fiancée and he was most agreeable. He even ventured that the sum involved would set him up with his own business premises. Apparently he has been quite worried that he won't be able to support you once you are married. And then there is the child of course."

"The child?"

"Oh, I thought I explained that. Yes, your child."

"But Joe and I don't have any children. Well not yet anyway."

"Maddy, you must learn to listen. The thing is that Joe is not going to be the father."

"Really, sir, you forget yourself."

"Joe is happy about the arrangement; in fact he encouraged me to speak to you about it as soon as possible to arrange the compensation. Now a lady like yourself, what would you want? Let me see, how about innocence, beauty, and immortality?"

"You mean I get to live for ever?"

"In a manner of speaking."

"What sort of manner?"

"You become the most loved, the most chaste, and the most oft-depicted woman in the whole world. Now that's not a bad deal is it?"

"So Joe gets the money, I get the fame, and you get my virginity?"

"Come, come. We both know you are no virgin – but let that pass, it will be as well to think of you thus."

"All the same, you get to give me one."

"We don't like to put it quite like that. Oh, and call me Gabe."

"So how do we put it, Gabe?"

"By the greatest good chance I have it all written down here."

He handed Maddy a parchment scroll that she studied intently. "OK, she said at last, I'm up for it. Where do I sign?"

Gabe bent over her, she started in response to the slight prick she felt on her right index finger. He pointed to the parchment and Maddy smeared her mark on it with her blood.

"Now we've only got time for a quickie, but you do understand the terms, don't you?"

Maddy nodded. Gabe turned her away from him and pulled her voluminous skirts up over her shoulders. "Best that you shouldn't see me," he explained. She felt a slight stirring, no more than that. It was over in a moment, in fact it hardly seemed to Maddy that she had been penetrated at all. She turned as soon as Gabe pulled her skirts down again and caught sight of him clipping shut a small wooden box.

"Blimey, Gabe, that wasn't much."

"Never mind that. We have just nine months to clean up your language, organise some good PR and get this show on the road."

He threw his cloak over his shoulders and started for the door.

"When will I see you again?" she said.

"I'm pretty tied up at present, but I'll send my man, Daniel. He's what I like to call an 'identity fixer'. You'll be a quite different person by the end of the year, and Dan will of course obliterate all that mucky past of yours. Got to dash – see you in nine months, if not before.'

"But what do you want me to do. Where will I have this baby?"

"Just come along here with Joe and we'll do the whole birth thing then. I've booked the room in advance."

Before he left the hotel Gabriel sought out the maître d. "That booking for the end of December. There'll be a bit of media interest. We'll need your very worst stable. Make it look as kitschy as you like – you know the sort of thing, some cattle, a grotty manger, some straw – oh yes, and see if you can round up some layabouts that will pass as shepherds. I'll handle the Kings."

"Certainly sir. May I enquire what you will be using it for?"

"If Madonna and Joseph get it right there will be at least a couple of millennia when the civilized world will say that the Son of God was born in your loose box, after that most of the profit will be in Christmas cards."

Riddle One

I have no personal feelings but am witness to much passion,
By nature I am dumb, but can tell a merry tale.
I will scratch and even nibble in the heat of the moment;
I am yours while you want me, but without you I will fail.

Sometimes I am golden, always easy-going,
My man-friends keep me safely to their heart.
My output speaks volumes, my habit is out-flowing,
And if you gently push me I'll help you make fresh start.

If I stray away or mess up I must ask you to forgive me,
Just take me in your hand and bring me back in line.
I know all your weaknesses, strengths, and aspirations
Your foibles and your secrets; yet you know none of mine.

You cannot say I'm wrong, because I'm always right,
And although I can wound others, for myself I feel no pain.
I am honest and deceitful, I am fickle and I'm true,
And another word for 'thoughtful' holds my name.

Riddle Two

We speak as one but are alone
We know no tunes but have a tone
Our Rules are Strict our Methods fair
If we are Up then have a care

Not quite Clapped out and with Appeal
Held captive in a wooden wheel
You stroke our Back and then our Hand
Give us a Round and then we'll Stand

In Sted-fast English, we were Found
Our hearts not oak, but just as Sound
We like to Hunt and often Course
But Changes are our tour de force

Royals and Minors throughout the land
Caters, or Majors make up our band
Swingers all, but very Sound
When we are Down we hang around.

Riddle Three

I am the strength of your platter
But when Spring your taste-buds go dead
In Classes I thrive if I'm fatter
But in Sets I am sent to my bed

I am your Golden Gourmet
On Camelot's fair isle
And Shah Jahan's sad story
Where my Purple roused his bile

If you tear at my skin I don't bellow
For its you that will tearfully cry
What's more it can turn things yellow
As soon as it boils – then I dye

I can make your libido feel tickled
But I'm floppy and green in your bed
Take me raw or stewed or pickled
Have me white or yellow or red

TOUCHING OTHERS

My skin is withered and peeling
I'm chopped and shredded and sliced
Or I'm silver and captive and reeling
In the wine they sponged up to Christ

A Breton may peddle with care
A necklace of me on a string
But as you unwrap me beware
For not I, but your eyes, will sting

Sonnet Makers

Poets write Sonnets to keep them amused
Sestinas and Clerihues help them play
Villanelles tend just to get them confused
Whilst Rondeaus will only lead them astray
Italian Sonnet form is quite bizarre
Spenserian rhythm seems a bit hard
But poets like me are happier by far
With the simpler rhyming scheme of the Bard

When as suggested our 'form be confined'
as we develop a poetic thread
I would concur when it brings to my mind
How Blank Verse would serve them much worse instead

So let Poetry flow, although we be
Confined by form, for in spirit we're free

The Old Disease

Clockwork regular,
stealing onwards nightly,
conferring Faustian favours
of deadly discontent.
Slipping by swiftly
from wingéd chariot,
the one-way arrow
of the Old Disease.

Detritus dermatology
best beguiled by Botox,
baby-bottom potions
caressing calloused curves.
Skin-deep remedies,
smoothing ever vainly
in cosmetic delusion
about the Old Disease

Gymnastic exertion
toning and honing,
muscling in on wasting,
wasting all the time.
Body parts rebelling with
over-stretched cramping,
knuckles gnarling
at the Old Disease

Shrunken horizons
now foreshortened,
yesterday's achievements
blurred to indistinction.
Darkening of days as
memory turns inwards,
with quiet capitulation
to the Old Disease.

The Voyeur

Just meandering. It is how I like to be. Nothing yet to focus upon, just spending a lazy afternoon in the sun. It is hot. I like that. My feet take me down the riverbank to the water's edge, into the river.

Flying things buzz at me in my idleness, but if I were to bother with them they would only be encouraged to pester me. I think they like my sweat but I am standing in this cool, cool river and have no need to sweat. In this summertime the water burbles slowly, intent upon its task of carrying this river to the sea.

Over by the blackthorn I can see a girl lying. She is pretty this girl, almost as pretty as an angel. Her hair is golden and her eyes blue. I lust after such angels as this. They come by once in a while, and I am waiting, waiting for them.

She holds a boy. She holds him tight. A dark-haired boy, he is as ugly as a wart-encrusted troll. They have their intentions. I have my intentions. I need to be just a shade closer to this unseeing pair I leave the cool of the water and stand with my head above the riverbank.. Watching is what I do; watching and after-things. This afternoon will be good watching. There will be good after-things.

The footpath is the other side of the hedge. The troll and my angel roll. They scrabble at each other. Clothes are removed. I see bodies. These two do not look to the river, they are too involved to see what might lurk on the riverbank, what might emerge from the river. I like involved. The troll has the fair maiden's breasts in both his ugly claws. He is grasping at them, squeezing them fit to milk, but there is no milk. The beautiful, beautiful angel gasps, groans and arches her back. I stand still and watch this. I enjoy watching. I feel detached from the action and yet in rhythm with it. I see such things quite often here. It is a good place for it, but not in winter. Winter is cover-up time for cocks and cunts. Strange really. You would think that it would be popular in winter. In winter buildings are better.

These water meadows are so familiar. I know every fold, every bit of brush, every mound, every smooth and welcoming hollow. As a sentinel above this curvaceous landform stands the church tower. A Saxon tower, it is round and upright. It is erect and firm and strong. It sounds of time and it sounds of bells and it sounds of dominance. It sounds better than the pub. I do not like the pub. There is too much noise, it is smelly and foul and surrounded by cars.

TOUCHING OTHERS

It is time for me to make my move. This is the best bit. This is where I get most satisfaction. It is likely to frighten them. I do have that effect, and I like it. This is what really turns me on. To quietly sidle up upon them in the fading of the evening light, or to accost them fast and fiercely in the heat of the day, a shadow bearing down on them with the strength of the sun behind it, now that really does it for me.

Then there are the nights. The nights are good, but are at their best when there is a half-moon. Then there are silver shadows over the meadow and silver shadows over the entwinings and silver shadows over my intentions. Then, in the silver shadows, it is not so dark that I cannot see, but it is not too bright to reveal me in full view.

Today the buttercups are the most beautiful of yellows. The buttercups wave at me kindly in this tease of breeze. I would like to wave back. But there are too many buttercups, and even I do not have that much time. I will be on my way, and the buttercups will be trodden and the yellow of the buttercups will be crushed and they will be broken buttercups.

I move.

I am naked.

I must reveal myself.

The beautiful siren starts to her feet with a cry of alarm, covering herself with her puny little hand. Her eyes are wide and her mouth drawn back in a rictus of alarm. This is good. This is the real orgasm of fear.

The troll makes to face me, but he is a worthless troll. He sees in me a power that he does not possess and will never possess. He is afraid, very afraid. The rictus strikes at him.

This angel is no angel now. Her straw coloured hair sticks flatly to her floppy breasts. I notice such intimates; they matter to me.

The troll has grabbed the fallen angel, the fearful angel, and is dragging it and his clothes away from me. But I am close – oh so close. My breath is in their nostrils. I smell their sweat, their fear. This is my moment, they are mine for the taking. I open my mouth in a paroxysm of fulfilment as my pent up lust overwhelms me.

Terrified they squeeze, half naked through the hedge and onto the footpath.

I hear the troll speak "That were a fucking Cow what bellowed at us," he says, "It's criminal."

"There ought t' be a soddin' law against letting fucking cows roam free in this field," says that which was my angel, my very, very fallen angel

I ruminate.

Purgatory

Being carried away, in solitary state,
to the place of the dying. Where live men hate
their deeds of destruction, the evil they've done,
fear victims they've vanquished, lose battles they've won.

They feel the tide's turning, now death draws so near
as their cold souls shrivel to slivers of fear.
But for others their dying means promise of rest
for Heaven 's for no one, not even the blest.

Oblivion enters and settles the score
taking us all, whether rich, whether poor;
ensuring that those who would walk with the Gods
will end up as Nitrogen – nourishing Sods!

Words of Times

Lughnasadh and Samhuin, Beltane and Imbolc;
A Celtic rural year dancing heathen Nordic tunes,
Bringing Slaughter and Salting, Sowing and Reaping,
Guising in the Sheiling, the reading of the Runes.
Fell and Force, Garth and Ghyll, Beck, and Cockley Crag,
Thwaite and Tarn, Syke and Howe, Lonnen, Yat, Dodd,
Thruff and Cam, Scrow, Rush, Gimmer, Twinter, Hogg;
The Yan, Tan, Tethera of the Norseman's homesick Trod.

Martinmas and Michaelmas, Lady Day and Lamas,
Candlemas and Christmas, Midsummers Day and Whit;
Haunting us, taunting us, as once familiar strangers,
Milestones of the year into Quarters carefully spilt.
Forest-won place-names: 'ham, and 'ton, and 'burgh;
Oxen-plough and Marl, Scythe, Stook and Loke and Loam,
Furlongs ploughed, Open Field, Stints on the Common;
Essential terms, tools, trades of the Saxon Harvest-home

Nanosecond Intel chip, Atomic Clock and i-Phone,
Rolex, Facebook, X, the commuting Groundhog Day.
Money laden Christmas-fest spilling back to August,
Strawberries in winter, Asynchronous Array.
Cyberspace and Digital, Queue and Quark, and Quantum,
Tesco, Azda, Morrisons, supply-chains on the road.
EasyJet and Ryanair queuing, packing, stacking;
Space-Time bending with inhuman over-load.

Brute

Drink not this cup purporting 'love'
For it may you defile
Its sweet-mouthed taste, its fragrant air
Does but conceal its bile

My words that flattered could deceive
Was evil their intent?
They cooed they preened they sought to groom
Was what they said quite meant?

Behind the charm of love's facade
Lies a twisted darkened place
Where demons stalk their gentle prey
whilst offering fond embrace

Such heartless hurt has sullied you
Defiled your love for me
Diminished something oh so good
With wanton cruelty

TOUCHING OTHERS

So take love's silver stake in hand,
My heart awaits your thrust.
Destroy this brute that lurks within
And claim the Love you trust.

Stuff

There is a man. The man lives in the house. The man is rich.

There is a woman. The woman lives in the house. The woman is scorned.

There is a door. The door leads to the kitchen. The kitchen is large.

There is a table. The table is in the kitchen. The table is made of wood.

The man has returned. He opens the door. The man enters the kitchen.

The woman looks to the door and to the man. There is no curiosity in the woman.

The man carries a package. He stoops to carry it. He places the package on the table. The man unwraps the package. He drops that wrapping.

Under the table there is a drawer. In that drawer there is a skewer. The skewer is sharp. The woman takes the skewer in her hand. It is her tool. She will use her tool.

The man and the woman do not speak. She tests the tip of the skewer. It is sharp.

TOUCHING OTHERS

The turkey has been plucked. The woman breaks the leg-bands. The legs spread.

There is stuffing. The man takes the stuffing. He stuffs the turkey. The turkey is bloated with the stuffing.

The woman pulls the legs together. The woman inserts the skewer. Using the skewer both legs are penetrated.

Blood oozes.

The legs hold in the stuffing.

*

Another table.

The man is the man. The man is not young.

There is a girl. The girl is pretty.

The man places the girl on the table. The man unwraps the girl, and drops her wrapping.

The girl is naked.

The girl is not curious. She is compliant.

The man has a tool. The girl takes the tool in her hands. The man and the girl do not speak. She feels the tool. It is hard.

The girl is on the table. Her legs are spread. The girl is ready for plucking.

The man plucks the girl.

Blood runs.

There is stuffing.

After the stuffing the girl pulls her legs together. The legs hold in the stuffing. Later the girl will be bloated from the stuffing.

The man is rich. Money talks.
The girl does not talk.

*

But the woman knows.

The man and the woman do not speak. The man knows that the woman knows.

There is a table. There is a drawer. In the drawer there is a knife

The woman takes the knife from the drawer.

She has a tool.

The woman looks at the knife.

The man looks at the knife.

The man is not curious. He is not compliant.

But there is penetration.

Blood flows.

Icarinism

Suddenly we fall,
my love,
suddenly we fall.
For a heart-splitting moment
before that
incomprehensible plunge
we sway, poised
on the knife-edge
of uncertainty.
And then
the balance swings
and, gathering momentum,
crashes to
the eternity of certainty.

Repairs Required

Warm water is seeping out from the underside of the white metal shroud of the boiler. It is running over my right hand and trickling down that arm to the elbow. I can't get the Mole Grips over the connection. Every time I try the bloody things slip. My arms ache from working above my head and the stream of metallic-smelling water is getting hotter.

"Bugger!" Swearing at it, and at my own incompetence, will do but little good, however chastising the thing is cathartic. In frustration I wallop the pipe with the Grips and it responds to such wanton brutality with a satisfying clang.

"You know that Christmas present that Andrew suggested we get for Rachael?" The voice enquires from the kitchen.

Christ – this is not the time to talk about Christmas presents. Now what bloody idiot put the boiler down here, almost on the floor, in the first place?

"Brian, I really need your help. Will you please listen to me and stop playing with that boiler."

TOUCHING OTHERS

My neck screams 'rest' at me, rebelling at the effort of holding my head at just the right angle so I can catch a glimpse of the offending piece of brass. Meanwhile, elsewhere, my left foot is toeing its way cautiously around something shallow that it's unexpectedly encountered. This container bears an uncanny resemblance to the cat litter tray.

"I've found just the thing online. I need you here to sort out the Internet when it screws up."

Please, not now. "Oh Fuck!" This latter as the Mole Grips finally recall their given purpose in the Great Scheme of Things and twirl the nut that final half turn necessary for it to part company with its threaded joint.

Much water flows. It 's hot.

"Brian, are you OK with that? Are you coming to help? Are you listening to me?"

I make a wild leap to escape this spouting geyser. My head hits the open access hatch, I try to steady myself but as my weight comes onto my left leg the litter tray – for it is indeed that – slides across the wet floor. The inevitable result is hot water, Mole Grips, cat-shit and me arranged over the utility room floor in the manner of a Paul Klee masterpiece.

"The thing is I really don't know whether to get her a 12 or a 14."

I roll onto my belly, wallowing in it, one hand over the end of the gushing pipe, like the

Dutch boy with his finger in the dyke, the other straining for the red-handled wheel-valve. A great stab of hot pain bores into my left palm.

"If we buy her a 12 and it's too small it will spoil the whole of Christmas."

My right hand gropes the valve. Hell, it just won't turn. I force my arm to twist it harder.

"On the other hand if we get a 14 and it's too large she will be mortified that we think she's that fat."

The valve cracks with an unexpected jolt, unbalancing me and yanking my retaining hand from the open-ended pipe. The boiler, having relieved itself of its burden of hot water, now sees its mission in life as being to drench me in a near-freezing deluge.

"So what do you think?"

I spin the valve shut.

"Brian, what should we do? I can't ask the girl, it is supposed to be a surprise present."

I stagger to my feet. My left palm is adorned with a bright red 28mm circle.

"Look, stop faffing about down there and talk to me. Honestly I do wonder sometimes; you really don't care about me do you?"

My jeans are at crisis point with the weight of water. A couple of careless steps and they will be relieved of existing duties to take up alternative residence around my ankles.

"You've never liked Rachael, right from the start. You always thought Andrew should have married Helen."

The place is awash with tepid water and cat faeces. It smells foul. I grab the mop and bucket and start bailing out.

"She's just not good enough for you is she? Just because she doesn't work in the city like Helen did."

Despite my exertions I am starting to shiver. The floor is damp now, rather than wet, and the smell of cat piss is following the lumpier bits of feline excrete down the outside drain.

"Well we can only hope you make it up to her properly this Christmas after that awful business last year. I hold you solely responsible for that, you know."

Warily I re-engage with floor, pipe and Mole Grips. With nothing to lose now I lie flat out on my back. My head is crammed underneath the boiler resting on the slightly smeary floor that is also hard and cold. At last I can see what I'm doing.

"Andrew behaved so well, considering what happened. And poor Rachael, just the memory of it makes me cringe. It's so good of them to come and see us again this year."

Got the bugger. The nut, no longer cross-threaded swarms up its thread like a homing pigeon and waits obediently whilst I apply binding torque with the Mole Grips.

"So probably best to go for the larger size, what do you say?"

I open the valve. There is the satisfying sound of whooshing water and the even more comforting knowledge that the joint is as tight as the Chancellor of the Exchequer.

"I can always hint that it is a little on the large size just in case there is a Good Reason early next year. Oh, Brian, that would be so lovely, wouldn't it?"

With the return of water pressure the boiler, with its distinctive rattle, fires itself noisily into life. Things, including me, should start warming up soon. A good bath, a hair-wash, a change of clothes, and I'll be just fine.

"Well if you don't want me to get it you can bugger off and buy her something else. Just carry on. I won't stop you. I don't see why I should be the only one who does all the work around here. You just don't love me, do you?"

Clipping up the access hatch I stand over the boiler, arms akimbo, triumphant in my conquest of all pipe-like things; just me and my trusty Mole Grips; together we can take on the whole world.

"Brian, what the hell have you been playing at?" says the figure in the doorway *"I've never seen such a mess and I don't believe you have listened to a word that I've been saying to you."*

War Babies

Into the terror of existence were we born
though the world then had not the time to mourn
the men who were dying, and would die,
in the five-year massacre of Versailles.

From that war on – because it exit in the rage
of an Atom bomb – life has been set on a stage,
and we, just as actors playing a part,
beguile our deeds with devious art.

We are living now in a world on the brink
of destruction, and find it hard to think
that if our leaders get one fact wrong
we have just four minutes to await the bomb.

It is for this reason that to no woman should man give
A few million spermatozoa, for one might live.
And although we may not think it wrong to seduce
let us accept that it is immoral to reproduce.

Underpass

Protagonist

I doubt you planned it should happen that way,
Though pickings powerful and trappings rich
Wed you to the Firm, but you did not stay
You simpering coy-faced, burdensome bitch.
Prince-shackled you strove to exert your will
Upstaging your hapless and tongue-tied mate.
You dressed yourself up and they snapped their fill,
A media frenzy of love and hate.

You produced your first son and then a spare.
You played with us, wooed us, kidnapping hearts,
You cuckolded him for whom you should care,
And there on telly you played Queen of Tarts.

Dead as a Dodi your days were a farce,
In life, as in death, a foul Underpass.

Antagonist

I was innocence, child-like purity,
Victim of Edinburgh, virgin not beast.
Lonely bride caged in harsh morality,
Engaging morsel for gross media feast.
My love was true, not "whatever that is",
Marriage holds two, but a mistress makes three.
My indiscretions: cries from a crisis
The Firm - as ice. The Horribilis - me.

Queen of Hearts broken, lost causes tended,
I was forced, divorced, and hung out to dry.
In the limelight with Harrods' intended
Playboy for play-girl was one in their eye!

Killing conspiracy breaks the impasse
Lets them ignore my life's sad Underpass

Sectioning

The hovering shimmers, ghostly in whiteness. Then a glinting, a familiarity; this is a thin point that I should know; floating quietly towards the side of me I can no longer see where it is. Perhaps I am frightened? Or is it an object of reassurance? I feel no insertion, but the white is fading. I am slipping back to grey.

Can I feel a Me, a proper, unflinchingly certain Me? Aha, we approach The Cogito do we not?

The grey is around me, it envelops me, consumes me. I become it.

Do you remember an Inn?

Could this be the something? Perhaps I am nearly there.

A plain, a great yellow plain, a deserted strand, stretches outwards, beckoning towards the far-off places, grasping after an ending. There is sky, an orange sky that flickers over that yellowness. Great misty grey clouds hang above the sky. They bellow.

TOUCHING OTHERS

*

As consciousness returned the colour started to regain his cheeks. His left arm clattered outwards, disturbing the bottle of saline drip so that it had to be steadied by a professional hand.

Duncan slowly opened his eyes. The world appeared to be shimmering slightly. He considered the proposition and decided that it was unlikely that there was something wrong with the world. Ergo his mental process was at fault. He needed more facts, and he needed them immediately.

He rolled his head to the left. Looming above him was a figure dressed in something blue, blue with a bit of white on it. He noted these facts and indexed them for storage.

Duncan was not afraid, but he was most certainly worried. He coughed a dry cough to attract the attention of Blue.

*

The plain contracts, not much, just its edges. The orange curls upwards. The clouds are clearer now. Discrete images move, not to some meteorological constant, or even to a pre-ordained pattern, but each to its individual whim. Do they have regard for each other? Are they truly free of will?

Prospero the magician, what did he beget?
Where the hell did that come from?

What is it trying to tell me? I am only just aware of this Me thing, but I have opened my eyes and the world is resolving itself. Separating out into Things Tangible and Things Ephemeral. To which of these can say Me to my I?

*

The nurse turned and smiled. "Ah, Duncan, welcome back to us, and how are we feeling?"

He looked at the blue-grey irises of this middle-aged woman. How irritating that he could not remember why he was here. What was he doing here, lying down in bed? And why was she speaking in the plural?

The facts were clear enough. He was in a hospital; he was sure of that. The bed was hard and single. Blue was a nurse. He brought his left arm back into his field of vision. There was a cannula inserted into his vein to which a saline infusion line was attached. He carefully recorded this information; it was clearly relevant to his present circumstance.

*

A moon swims into focus.
Is it a moon that I search? If so, then where is it? Not our moon, not Earth's Moon. So what is my moon?

The shadows quake and roar again, but I can discern between them, they have different cadences. There is speaking, that is what it is. I listen to the hum and the patter of the words. They fall light upon my ears and trickle with a gentle insistence from thence to my brain.

There is a person. I see a Galatea, a neo-Galatea perhaps; thus the inanimate is animated.

*

"Where am I? What's happened to me?"

"Now don't you go upsetting yourself, Duncan. We're here in Recovery, and we're fine."

"No. I'm not fine. What's happened to me?"

"Just our little procedure, dear."

"What procedure? What are you telling me?"

"We'll be as right as rain soon, dear, just relax."

"There's something on my head."

"Just a bandage, don't worry about it. It all went very well they tell me."

"What went well?"

Duncan closed his eyes against this in-rush of information. He needed to file. OK, filing now. Some terrible accident must have befallen him; he must have been knocked out. An ambulance would have brought him to casualty. He had, presumably, suffered some sort of head injury. He tried to remember what he'd been doing that morning, but those drawers in the filing cabinet were stuck fast. He would have to wait.

He opened his eyes. Blue-grey was still watching him. "When can I go home?"

"We'll just have a little rest, dear. We can ask Doctor as soon as she's here. She won't be long."

*

'Wonderful'. 'Strange'. 'Admired'.

Now I am a dictionary, no not a dictionary, a thesaurus. Hardly even a thesaurus, but a reference to mythology. A mythological thesaurus trying to find the answer.

There are too many references. And yet I strive. I strive through them. I strive a name. It is a name I must have. Tarantella, that's it: *'The spreading and the tedding of the straw for a bedding'*,

I grin.

The answer is indeed in the very first line of that poem; also a moon of Uranus; and a daughter of Prospero, finally a word that means wonderful, strange, or admired.

Why do I need to know this? A dread creeps. A deep, dark shadow crosses my path and, metaphorically, I shiver.

I feel a touch upon me. I open my eyes. A nurse stands there with her hand resting on my shoulder.

"We were shaking, dear."

Not so metaphorical then. She is middle-aged with clear blue-grey eyes. She looks worried.

"Where am I?"

"Like I said, we're in Recovery. Now we should get some rest. Doctor will be along shortly."

"Have I been badly hurt?"

"Like I said before before. We just have a bandage around our head."

"No you didn't."

"Didn't what?"

"You didn't 'tell me before' about that."

The nurse shakes her head slightly. I seem to worry her although I have no idea why that might be. She is pretty, this nurse, with golden curls. Beyond her curls the room is bleak and Magnolia. There are hinged metal things clinging to the walls like giant limpets, embarrassed by their nakedness. She of the golden curls looks at each of my pupils in turn. She looks more perplexed than worried now. She makes a note on a card she is holding.

"We just need to rest, dear, Doctor will come shortly."

*

He watched carefully. The Doctor must have been her doing her rounds. She was young, this one, hardly thirty. He knew that he knew her. She wore a white coat. There were two others with her including Blue. The other had more white than blue. Duncan noticed these things. They were things for filing away.

The Doctor was listening carefully to the nurses, pausing for discussion with each them, and that was good. Except it was taking ages for her to get around to talk to him. Never mind, he had plenty to do. He started to pull drawers at random, searching frantically for recognition. She was there somewhere; of that he was certain.

Duncan considered what the hell he must look like. He would take some rip from his colleagues. He would need to counter that. He smiled slightly.

"Glad to see you smiling Dunc."

"Not sure I have that much to smile about. Are you going to let me out?"

He looked carefully at this competent Doctor. Her face was as familiar as if he had seen it on the far side of his breakfast table this morning.

Miranda was looking at Duncan's notes. She had a quiet word with Blue.

"You're a bit more confused than we would have expected."

"I don't feel in the least confused."

"You keep asking Nurse the same questions."

"That I can't recall."

"Well I think we need to carry out a few tests just to make sure that everything is as it should be. Do you remember how we discussed the possibility?"

With that Miranda stooped down and shone a small light into each of Duncan's eyes.

*

The light is blinding me; then again in the other eye. I focus properly as the face of a woman clad in a white housecoat pulls away from mine.

"No sign of any concussion. But all the same we need to keep you here."

Have I missed something? Was I dozing? What the hell is going on?

"Who are you? Are you the doctor?"

"Don't you know me?" She is looking rather puzzled, also just slightly pleased with herself. I have no idea why.

"Am I OK to go? I know I'm a bit confused, but I'm sure I'll be just fine."

"You just said you were not confused."

'Nonsense."

"Dunc, you are doing so well. It is almost exactly as we had hoped. The interesting thing is to see what happens after a day or two."

Miranda turns to Golden Curls and talks seriously to her for a full minute. She then makes a note on my record sheet. She is just a couple of metres away.

"Is there a problem?"

It seems an innocent enough question, but my Lady sans Lamp declines to hear it. She turns towards me.

"Can you remember what happened to you?"

"No."

"And my name?"

My thoughts wander at random, playing with poems, planets and the Bard. "Miranda?"

*

Duncan needed to be sure. Things like this should never be left to chance. He had the drawer open now, the one he had carefully labelled 'wife'. He had cross-referenced that this was his. "Doctor."

Miranda turned.

"I am sure that you are my wife."

Miranda looked at him with a detached air, clearly assessing him and the immediate state of his consciousness. "That's true."

"And you are called Miranda, and we had breakfast together this morning."

"That's also correct."

Duncan was opening filing drawers as

fast as he could. He found it. "And we agreed that I should go through with this?"

*

As they left the room the Nurse turned to Miranda. "Will your husband be any trouble now?"

"Partial sectioning of the corpus callosum is a tricky procedure, even under Laboratory conditions, but I now have all the advantages of polyandry without the criminal drawback. One body containing two husbands, one right-brain, the other left-brain."

"If you don't mind me asking," said the Nurse, "what made him agree to it?"

"He was in a bad way. The choice was being sectioned or being Sectioned."

Suffice

When he comes
she is there,
likewise.
No words slip
the silence
to intrude
between
their dreams.
Assuredly
there is nothing
save this.
And it
will
suffice.

Archived

Sole guardian now of my poor creations,
formless record of a lifetime of facts,
protectively pooling past sensations,
a jumbled imagery of ancient acts.
Hollow echo of a life so fleeting,
On this frail catacomb must I rely,
amidst final twitch of thought retreating,
for faint cheating chance, that mind will not die.

Dead brain-matter lies denuded, useless,
that which defined me will go where it must,
death's perfection, so complete and faultless,
renders all intelligence back to dust.

Where once I was are just memories of me,
granting me chance of immortality.

The Times of my Life

Fluid for swirling
Blood for warming
Heartbeat for comforting
Cord for succoring
I am having the time of my life

Teat for sucking
Mother for loving
Nappies for shitting
Arms for embracing
I am having the time of my life

Friends for playing
Conkers for winning
Hair for pulling
Knees for mudding
I am having the time of my life

Bodies for fucking
Cars for racing
Parties for raving
Causes for marching
I am having the time of my life

Spouse for loving
Children for playing
Job for working
Mortgage for paying
I am having the time of my life

Booze for drinking
Abroad for going
Partner for cheating
Money for everything
I am having the time of my life

Chair for sitting
Family for framing
Aches for doctoring
Days for recalling
I am having the time of my life

Bells for tolling
Coffin for carrying
Graveside for weeping
Body for rotting
I have had the time of my life.

Her Character

Her long black silky hair defines her features, framing her face and falling in waves down her back. Oh what hair, enticing a longing to run your fingers through it, to caress it, to see the excitement in her eyes as it ripples through your hands.

She possesses such an exuberant nature, totally outgoing, and is friendly almost to a fault. Invariably the first to tackle any situation and never chastened if things don't turn out exactly as expected. She is such a loyal friend, perhaps more than a friend. Not given to an excess of talking she exhibits a rare sensitivity to the concerns of others.

Then there are those beautiful light brown eyes, set so deeply behind long black lashes. That old cliché 'windows to the soul' springs to mind, but then the Church would have it that Flatcoated Retrievers do not possess anything so intangible as a soul.

Saga

An ode to Saga, a much-loved dog,

Remember me in the summer sun,
    high larks singing,
The rushing beck, the heather-scent,
    the open moor inviting,
The endless days, the ripening wheat,
    the bat-studded gloaming,
The hay-time lates, the velvet nights. . . . .
    As a cloud shadow passing.

Remember me in the Autumn mists,
    sharp game-birds rising,
The web-draped hedge, the cartridge smell,
    the wild wind storming,
The clarty plough, the rain-cold kale,
    the days-end towelling,
The orchard glut, the harvest-home . . . . .
    With a 'gone away' a' blowing.

Remember me in the snow-filled lane,
    the laden boughs drooping,
The crackling lake, the rook-stark trees,
    the bird-bath-braking,
The beet-mud road, the toasting fork,
    the lantern-hung caroling,
The warming hearth, the cheering cup.......
    As a Yule Log burning.

Remember me in the bud-burst spring,
    the leafing and the flowering,
The green-tipped field, the gamboling lambs,
    a chorus sung at morning,
But grieve you not with saddened heart,
    the time was mine – for passing,
My life was good, so remember me.....
    in each new life that's dawning.

ABOUT THE AUTHOR

Well, yes, that's me, Gordon.

What should I write about myself that could be of conceivable interest to anyone at all - whether they know me or not. I mean you have arrived here, I hope, to read some of my poems and short stories, and I don't know about you but it is sometimes a real let-down to actually meet the person whose tales you have been enjoying - an awful disappointment.

A product of my Alma Mater, Evelyn Waugh, said when asked if he were educated at Lancing College "No, I was at school there." That sums up my opinion of the place as well. I have fonder memories of my prep school, Orwell Park where a wonderful English teacher 'O-D' encouraged me to write.

My parents owned a private pack of hunting beagles, and were kind enough to appoint me as First Whip. Strange that such sport is illegal now, mind you there are an awful lot of things that are illegal in England that I find irksome - but I had better not start on that or you may be minded to report me to the Thought Police for stepping over the line.

So I could tell you that I used to fly planes, race cars and sail boats - but why on earth would you be interested in that - anyway I did none of those things particularly well. I could

ABOUT THE AUTHOR

tell you that I was the Regional Agent for The National Trust first in North Wales and then in the Nothwest of England. I could tell you that I left the NT and established and ran a successful passenger boat business on Coniston Water. All the above is desperately uninteresting!

Perhaps you might like to know that for most of my life I have owned dogs - Labradors, Golden Retrievers, but most especially Flatcoated Retrievers. But that is really between me and them and probably does not say much about my character. I suppose you could be interested to know that now I spend a large part of my life in Northern Greece (Thessaloniki and Halkidiki), and still have a small cottage in Northern England.

But if I were you I would politely ignore all the foregoing and just enjoy such poems and stories as may appeal you.

Gordon
Halkidiki
June '24

www.ingramcontent.com/pod-product-compliance
Lightning Source LLC
Chambersburg PA
CBHW020426010526
44118CB00010B/449